Behind Blue Eyes

Shannon Palmo

BookLeaf Publishing

Presentation by *BookLeaf Publishing*

Web: www.bookleafpub.com

E-mail: info@bookleafpub.com

ISBN: 9789357214414

First edition 2022

To Michael,

Thank you for supporting and encouraging me to make my dream a reality and believing in me to make it come true.

PREFACE

To see into the mind of someone who struggles with mental health can be eye opening. Seeing how just one event or one thing can spin in their mind. How love, loss and more can send a person into darkness or light.

Seeing Is Believing

"Seeing is believing"
Or so I've been told
But what of seeing is believing?
From what I have seen: of life itself
What you see is not always,
What it appears to be
As you grow, life appears.
Death
          Life
                    Rebirth
Allapartoflife
See the birth of a baby
The death of an elder
See the plants die then come to life in spring
The child playing
All of which you believe because you see!
Yet can be unbelievable
That child may not be playing but
                                        Creating

Learning
The death of an elder
          Could be the birth of a baby
And yet what we see is what we see
Therefore we believe
What has been seen

Waking Up

Waking up
It's a new day
New adventures
New people
What to do?
Join a circus
Be a star
Who to become?
A writer
Musician
What to do?
Where to go?
Tothemoonandback
Venus
Mars
Life: IT HAPPENS
Then you F
A
L
L
Into a dark hole
F
A
L
L

…………………………

"WAKE UP!"

Its over.

Nature Reborn

The past few months have seen nature reborn
While humans are forced to stay inside
To not travel
We are seeing the most astounding changes
around us
Venice, Italy is seeing clear water ways
Jelly fish are swimming in the waters
And for once we can see them
There is no boat traffic
Polluting the waters
Cities are seeing clear sky's
As air pollution is down
Due to lack of planes and cars driving around
Nature is healing
While we are home
It is astonishing what can happen
When nature is not affected by humans
It can heal
And be reborn

Stigmas

We live in a world full of stigmas
Stigmas with Mental Health, Schooling, and
Body Image
These are just three examples
The three main stigmas that my life is
surrounded in
My whole life I have been in a box
"Just get over it; your mental issues are all in
your head, everyone deals with the same things
and still live their lives"
"You should be done with school by now"
"Your gaining weight, when will you be starting
the diet"
The main three sayings I hear daily
But I still push against these stigmas
Constantly advocating for the stigmas around
these topics
Too many ignorant people
Refusing to admit there is a problem
A problem with suicide
Mental Health
A problem with setting a time limit with
school
Graduating high school

Getting your college
degree
A problem with body image
What you should look like
How you should dress
Eating disorders
to match your mental health
All these things
Yet no one wants to acknowledge
I fight the stigmas in my life
They are a part of me
And people should be more open
Not ignorant
I've made it my mission
To educate
To eliminate
Stigmas

Duet of Siblings

Growing up I had two brothers
But alas one brother was separated
And it was myself and my brother
Raised in one house
We grew up as one
One year and 16 days apart
Almost makes my Gemini a prophet
As we were often mistaken for twins
And many times
On vacations
We pretended we were twins
Knowing that the kid we met
We'd never see again
Growing up
We were close
Always playing together
Getting into the N64
Placing bets
        On who would win at mario kart
Even as we got older
While in different friend groups
We still came together
My brother's friends and mine
All hanging out
Both my brother and I

Always protecting each other
NOW
I don't know why he's not around
I have my suspicions
But don't understand
How two siblings
Once close
Can become
Complete strangers.

Dream

I cry in her 2013 blue cobalt
I had run past my schools
Baseball game happening between middle school and high school math and social studies teachers
I yelled "Nan! Wait up"
She turned to me, and we got in the car
She started speaking "I need you to be ready for when I leave you again and allow yourself to grieve and move forward"
I cried "why does it feel like I AM the only person who's allowed myself to feel your gone"
Nan said "pop doesn't know how to handle you kids. You were dropped on us and I took care of it all. Now I'm gone and he doesn't know how to help."
The dream fades as I keep sobbing
Until the same one forms
I find myself running towards where her car just was previously
Waiting and waiting
While characters from the TV shows form
One asks
"What's wrong child"
I tell her I'm waiting

She should be pulling up any minute
She just did
But this time she’s gone
She doesn’t show and a nightmare begins.
Eventually I wake
Wanting to fully capture our conversation
Only to fall back to sleep
And wake an hour later
And only a vague idea about her words.
Damn it.

The Singer

From a young age I was trained to sing
Sitting at a piano with my Nana playing
Singing with her as she played each song
Growing up all I wanted to do was sing
Listening to my favorite musicians
Coming up with dance moves while I sang
All done in my bedroom
I sang with my nana every weekend until she left
I began singing in the school and church choirs
Eventually only continuing to sing in the school
choir
My dream was to sing and be on stage
While my Nana encouraged me
My grandparents did not
To them it was not practical
Something unrealistic
My high school also silenced my voice
Eventually I became scared to sing alone
Even knowing I had an amazing voice
My grandparents and my choir teacher's voices
and actions rang clear
I cannot make it
And then the favoritism in the choir were
discouraging
I am now almost 31

I still sing to my heart's content
Although now I sing for me
I have learned to sing in roughly 7 different languages
But the voices I hear now
Are still the same
I still have stage fright
And will only sing around people I am comfortable with
But to me that is ok
Because music is the best therapy
And will always be important to me.

What Brings Out The Worst In People

What brings out the worst in a person?
A question I have been pondering as of late
Currently we live in a world where we as humans are
Stuck in our homes
Forced to wear masks when we go out
Unable to see loved ones
A Pandemic of epic proportions
Corona Virus or COVID- 19
Nothing quite seen for many of us
I am what is now called an essential worker
Working in customer service
I have seen many things in my many years in this industry
Always seeing something that leaves me speechless
But
It is now that I am seeing the worst in humanity
While many praise our health care workers
And other essentials
I am seeing the worst

I have always thought people couldn't ever get worse
Until now,
Many people who come into the store I work at are
Rude
Ignorant
Entitled
And many more words that at the moment I can't find
I am hearing all these people complain
Watching as myself and my co-workers respond with sarcasm ourselves
Just because of how people act
I have had customers rip items out of my hands
I have been called names that I have to do a double take
And most of all
I have seen the most disrespectful people
And I am dumbfounded
Thinking
Wondering
How people can act like this
During a time like this
I am witnessing
The worst in humankind
While there are people who are just as kind and considerate
As there are the complete opposite

I didn’t expect a pandemic
To bring out the worst in people.

Time

I take the time
I take the time to write
Each word
Precise and meticulous on the page
I take the time for people
To spend time with
To be with
I don't care for material possessions
For time is my currency
I always value time
You never know how much on has left
Time
Such a simple concept
Words
So valuable and yet taken for granted
I take the time
The question is
Are you worth it?

To Give Up One Life For Another

I've recently been looking back on childhood
Adolescence
and adulthood
I look at my grandparents, especially my grandmother
I am thinking back on everything since her passing only months ago
It feels like just yesterday she was here but also feeling like it's been forever
Her and my grandfather decided 25 years ago to forgo their own lives
To raise children that were not their own
They had raised their children
And now chose to raise two grandchildren
They could have left us with our parents
And let them fight it out and figure out custody arrangements
But they saw innocence and decided what was best for us,
was a stable home life
While they took in two out of three children
Mainly because the third was destructive and was sent back to our parents

They still decided to take us in
Instead of living their own lives
We were raised on morals and chores
In the summer we vacationed at the beach
Getting up early to find seashells
Or riding bikes on the boardwalk
Going on the rides at night and playing games
They took us to dance
sporting practice and events
and everything in between
Instead of being grandparents to us
They were our parents
They worked while we were in school
Came home to make dinner and get us in bed
Made sure we didn't go without
Or want for nothing
What was supposed to be their life
Their money
Their time
Became ours
They gave up a life together, alone with no children
But the grandkids that would come along
To raise someone else's kids
Even now to this day, 30 years later
My grandfather continues to help and care for us
When we need him
Although now it is us who are looking after him
He is more than capable to be on his own

But he lost his love
And is now learning to live on his own,
Alone with the dog
We return the favor of checking in on him
Helping if he wants it
Making sure he is doing ok
I helped him in the last 10 years with taking care of my grandmother
Returning the favor of caring for two people who cared for me
I stay close by, knowing he will be ok, but not wanting to leave him
His wife of 40 some years gone
And I think of the sacrifices they made
And I am thankful for that and them
They gave up their lives to be parents to children that were not theirs
I can only imagine the life they could have had
If they had not switched it for another.

Welcome to the Pandemic

Welcome to quarantine
Welcome to sickness
Welcome to distance
Welcome to the current world pandemic
Families unable to see each other
Individuals who live alone stuck in an empty home
People scared because they a considered immune compromised
People who are essential and immune compromised
Still having to go to work and risk illness
Welcome to a world where we see humanity at its worse
And yet I see something else
I am immune compromised
I am an essential worker
But I am not thinking of myself
I am thinking of my grandmother
I am thinking of the many emotions surrounding me
Happy, Relief, Sadness
It was just 6 months ago we lost her
I think about everything happening now

And know that she wouldn't have made it
through this pandemic
As much as I miss her, I think she was better off
to have passed when she did
I don't think of myself
I think of my mom and grandfather
Both who if they get sick, it could kill them
Even though like me they have compromised
immune systems
I think about the positives of life right now
Our planet healing from all of the toxicity of
humans
Seeing side by side photos of Venice Italy
One photo with a boat and the other without boat
traffic
I see our planet becoming more alive
We still have a long way to go
But some good is coming of this
I post random memes and lists
Just to get a smile on at least one persons face
I am choosing to not let fear take over me
Those with anxiety, not freaking out
We've already imagined the worst so this is
nothing to us
But the choice to not let fear take over
That is hard especially with all we read and see
I still would rather be silly and keep everyone's
spirits up
This is my choice

Maybe more should make the same choice
Let the fear dissipate into hope.

Dancing of the Mind

Tears glistening
As her mind dances
Around everything
And nothing at all
She suffocates
As her mind keeps moving
Grasping for air
Wanting peace
But the dance is ongoing
She is up and down
First position
Second
Third
Fourth
And Fifth
And arabesque
Next, she is on her toes
Spinning
Round and round, she goes
Constantly trying for perfection
The same routine
Every day with the dancing, her mind does
Wanting to feel how she felt
When she danced
So light and full of air

But her mind is a tricky place
Always worrying
Always
SOMETHING
So instead of dancing
She cries
Wishing for life to be as it was
When she was just a little girl
Learning how to dance.

In My Own Little Corner

In my own little corner
In my own little chair
Sun shines through my window
I'm lost in a book
Pretending I am somewhere other than here
I often find myself wishing
Wishing I am someone else
The corner where I sit
Sometimes reading
          Sometimes looking out the window
Allowing my mind to run wild
Mostly wishing I was like everyone else
No mental health issues
          No trauma

Just normal.
Pretending I am in my books
Living as the characters do
Wondering what my life would be like
Had I been born
          Different
                    Into another family
Even so
I know in my own little corner
In my own little chair
I can be whoever I want to be

Hope in Darkness

In the world we live in
To find beauty in darkness
Seems almost impossible
Every day of our lives
We see
Death
Hate
Crime
So much so it is easy to lose hope
But in these dark times
We also see
Birth
Love
Community
All that can give us hope
Hope that not all of humanity is lost in the darkness
The sun rises everyday
Rain or Shine
Each season brings something new and beautiful
In its own way
There is always a little faith
If you know how to see
Through all the darkness
That little glimmer of Hope
Is always shining through

Missed

To go on a journey into the wilderness
All alone with no one but myself
The things I'd miss would be immense
I'd miss my mother
Her cooking
Warm embrace
Her loving voice and laughter
I'd miss my family
The Birthdays
Parties
The little things my cousins and siblings do that seem too funny to be true
I'd miss
My space
My bed
My books
My art supplies
Every comfort my home holds
While I can survive the wilderness
Only from camping with my father and brothers as a kid

I'd end up missing more by being gone, more than a week
I'd miss everything in my daily life
Only because being alone in the wilderness with just my thoughts
Is even more terrifying than the wilderness itself

Phases

Like the moon across the sky
Every night a different phase
Such the same in life
The phases we go through
From birth to death
We are always changing
Our Style
Our Personalities
Our thought processes
Always phasing from one thing to the next
Like the moon across the night sky
We deal with the darkness within us
And try to shine bright in that darkness
We are always changing who we are
Into who we want to be
From one phase to the next
Until we are finally full and new
Then we change once more
Into what we need to be next

Remembering Ugly Yet Beautiful Items

Cleaning and organizing the basement in my grandparents' home
My grandmother in a chair helping me organize their stuff
Coming across old items passed down to her from her mother
She says to donate them
I respond with a no
"These were handmade by your mother; not something you just get rid of" I say
Remembering the Christmas, the year before when we went through old photos and her tearing up
We continue to organize the clutter of things
Slowly she realized I was right
And begins to start telling me about each item
I learn more about her mother
Who had hand painted and made many of the trinkets we find
Slowly she is convinced to keep some of the items
Reminiscing about each item we find
Telling me to donate or keep
Much of it I fought her to keep

Knowing the sentimental values
Even some that were broke
I say we keep it, I can fix it
We spent a good two hours or so
Going through the boxes
Creating two donation boxes
I feel proud of myself
Knowing I broke down my grandmother's hard shell
Getting her to keep the old antiques and items from her mother
I knew my argument was sound

"If you get rid of this, you'll regret it knowing you can pass it down; but that its your mothers.

I know I would hate to lose or get rid of something that reminded me of you when you're gone"

With that she listened
And we continued.

The Collection

Sitting in my living room
Looking at my two book cases
Admiring the number of books, I've collected
over the many years of my life
All organized
By Author
Series
Genre
Knowing I've only read half of what I own
Always buying more books
New worlds to explore
New ideas and concepts to think about
In between my book cases
Stand my entertainment stand
That holds all my movies, my TV, Blu Ray
Player and Internet boxes
I think about the movies in the cabinets and the
ones visible on the shelf
Again, admiring how much I've collected over
the years
These how ever are not organized the same way
as my books
But are organized by
Genre and Series
With the one cabinet having all my TV series

I admire both my collections
Knowing that they will always be a good
investment
As my family believes I should stop buying
books and movies
And get rid of what I have
I always protest
And in that protest, I say
"One of these days the internet or cable will be
down, and I will have all my movies to watch to
keep me busy"
Their counter argument to that being
"Well if the internet and cable is down then
there's not power or electricity most likely"
Again, I look at them with my smug look
And just say
"That's what books are for"
Knowing I always will win when it comes to
justifying my collection of books and movies
Always looking at them and admiring them
The vast and endless possibilities
And all I can learn from them all

Fear

What scares you the most?
What haunts your dreams to the point that they are reality?
I'm not just talking about the usual scares
The Clowns
Spiders
Darkness
People
People are what scare me the most
Nothing is more terrifying than humankind
Killing others dreams, hopes
Our humanity
I fear people
I fear being let down
Let go
Destroyed more than has already been
It's people who hurt you the most
There's a constant game being played
One that everyone else knows is being played but you
I fear being in love
Because what I've been shown for giving love
Is my heart cut out, and diced into so many pieces?
It's impossible to put back together

I fear trusting someone
Because my trust has been destroyed
I fear letting people in
Because they all seem to leave
It's people who have turned me into
this scared little creature
And it was I who allowed some of it to happen
So, what is it I fear most?
Letting you in, and being let go of and down
People are the real monsters
Tell me should I be afraid of you?

Freedom

Sitting here thinking
Crying
Wondering if I'll ever be free
Free of control
Free to find myself again
A girl who has lost her way
Someone drowning in sorrow
Nothing but pain and agony is felt
Thinking the death of one would set me free
Only to shackle me down once again by another
How is one supposed to find the person?
        They were
            They want to be
If no one gives them the freedom to do so
I have to conceal
Don't feel
And let everyone think I'm ok
Put on a brave face for everyone
Except
What about me
When do I get to be free?
Free to feel
Free to do as I please
Where's my happy ending
When will I finally see the freedom?
I've so longed for all these years.

The Boy Who Took Away The Shadows

What does it mean to feel joy?
To me it's a strange concept
Something I hardly ever feel
Mostly because whenever I feel
Joy
Happiness
It is taken away swiftly
I feel as though it has been ages since such sensations were felt
The purest form of joy I can remember feeling left
June 2017 is the last time I felt something so pure
He had been a part of my life for so many years
When I was with him the whole world melted away
It was just him and I
Together
No one else
His embrace
His touch
His voice
Him in general
Was like a melody playing

It was love
It was serenity
We were comfortable with each other
He accepted everything about me
    Good and Bad
And I the same
    Until everything changed
The change hit me like a freight train
I was blindsided and confused
To this day; two years later
That pain is still there
And I have yet to feel that same pure joy
    And happiness again

www.ingramcontent.com/pod-product-compliance
Lightning Source LLC
Chambersburg PA
CBHW051743130826
49812CB00033B/985
9789357214414